THE BOOK OF

Deuteronomy

ONE CHAPTER A DAY

GoodMorningGirls.org

Welcome to Good Morning Girls! We are so glad you are joining us.

God created us to walk with Him, to know Him, and to be loved by Him. He is our living well, and when we drink from the water He continually provides, His living water will change the entire course of our lives.

> *Jesus said: "Whoever drinks of the water that I will give him will never be thirsty again. The water that I will give him will become in him a spring of water welling up to eternal life." ~ John 4:14 (ESV)*

So let's begin.

The method we use here at GMG is called the **SOAK** method.

- ❏ **S**—The S stands for *Scripture*—Read the chapter for the day. Then choose 1-2 verses and write them out word for word. (There is no right or wrong choice—just let the Holy Spirit guide you.)

- ❏ **O**—The O stands for *Observation*—Look at the verse or verses you wrote out. Write 1 or 2 observations. What stands out to you? What do you learn about the character of God from these verses? Is there a promise, command or teaching?

- ❏ **A**—The A stands for *Application*—Personalize the verses. What is God saying to you? How can you apply them to your life? Are there any changes you need to make or an action to take?

- ❏ **K**—The K stands for *Kneeling in Prayer*—Pause, kneel and pray. Confess any sin God has revealed to you today. Praise God for His word. Pray the passage over your own life or someone you love. Ask God to help you live out your applications.

SOAK God's word into your heart and squeeze every bit of nourishment you can out of each day's scripture reading. Soon you will find your life transformed by the renewing of your mind!

Walk with the King!

Courtney

WomenLivingWell.org, GoodMorningGirls.org

Join the GMG Community

Share your daily SOAK at 7:45am on **Facebook.com/GoodMorningGirlsWLW**

Instagram: WomenLivingWell #GoodMorningGirls

GMG Bible Coloring Chart

COLORS	KEYWORDS
PURPLE	God, Jesus, Holy Spirit, Saviour, Messiah
PINK	women of the Bible, family, marriage, parenting, friendship, relationships
RED	love, kindness, mercy, compassion, peace, grace
GREEN	faith, obedience, growth, fruit, salvation, fellowship, repentance
YELLOW	worship, prayer, praise, doctrine, angels, miracles, power of God, blessings
BLUE	wisdom, teaching, instruction, commands
ORANGE	prophecy, history, times, places, kings, genealogies, people, numbers, covenants, vows, visions, oaths, future
BROWN/GRAY	Satan, sin, death, hell, evil, idols, false teachers, hypocrisy, temptation

Introduction to the Book of Deuteronomy

Deuteronomy is known as the long farewell speech of Moses and the second giving of the law. The nation of Israel had spent 40 years wandering in the desert. The old generation had all but died off and would not enter the Promised Land. Now, a younger generation would go in, to claim the promises that God had made to their forefathers.

Moses wanted to remind the Israelites of the law that God had given them. The tone is different from the first giving of the law in the book of Exodus. Now, the tone is one legacy and love. The heart is that the children of Israel - and us today - would obey God because we love Him. We need to teach our children - and our children's children- to love God and obey Him also.

God had done so many great things. They had experienced his love and protection. The children of Israel should have had no problem following him. They knew His expectations to obey. They had learned the holiness of God and that because of His holiness they too should be holy.

Purpose: To remind Israel what God had done and to help them rededicate their lives to Him. For us, we can be reminded of the loving kindness of our God and renew our commitment to love and obey Him.

Author: Moses. Although it is said that the end of the book, where it gives the account of Moses' death, might have been written by Joshua.

Time Period: The book was written to Israel around 1407 BC.

Key Verses: "You shall love the LORD your God with all your heart and with all your soul and with all your might. 6 And these words that I command you today shall be on your heart. 7 You shall teach them diligently to your children, and shall talk of them when you sit in your house, and when you walk by the way, and when you lie down, and when you rise." Deuteronomy 6:5-7

The Outline:

1. **What God has done for us** (1:1-4:43)
   This is Moses' first address.   Moses reviews the mighty acts of God for the nation of Israel.

2. **Principles of Godly Living** (4:44-28:68)
   Obeying God's law brought blessing and disobeying brought misfortune. In this section we see:

   - ❏ The Ten Commandments
   - ❏ The command to love the Lord your God
   - ❏ Laws for proper worship
   - ❏ Laws for ruling the nation
   - ❏ Laws for human relationships
   - ❏ Consequence for obedience and disobedience

3. **A Call for Commitment to God (29:1-30:20)**
   God's covenant to His people is renewed in Moab and God's people are called to love and obey God.

4. **The Change in Leadership: (31:1-34:12)**
   Moses made mistakes, yet he was still a good leader and carried out God's commands.

Deuteronomy has much for us to learn as well. We can be reminded that God is involved in every area of our lives. We are reminded that obedience and disobedience carry inevitable consequences. God is still calling us to be committed to Him today. We can also learn that we all make mistakes but God can still use us despite our mistakes and those mistakes should not stop us from living with integrity and a commitment to godliness.

There are five major themes in the book of Deuteronomy:

History: Moses reviews the mighty acts of God. This is important for us because we should remember the great and wonderful things that God has done in our lives in the past. This is part of His character and His character is unchanging. We know god more intimately by knowing his character and remembering what He has done in our lives.

Laws: God reviewed his law for the people. Commitment to God and his truth can't be taken for granted. We need to remember that we are passing on the words of God to future generations.

Love: God's faithful and patient love is portrayed. God shows his love by being faithful. God's love forms the foundation of our trust in him. We can trust Him because He has proven Himself faithful.

Choices: God reminds his people that they must choose the path of obedience. Our choices make a difference. Choosing to follow God benefits our relationship with God and others.

Teaching: God commanded the Israelites to teach their children his ways. We need to be teaching our children God's ways. It must be a priority. More than teaching tradition, we must teach that loving God begins in our heart and minds.

 This book reminds me of the old hymn titled Trust and Obey. It says, "Trust and obey, for there's no other way, to be happy in Jesus but to trust and obey."

May we see the love that the Lord has for us and may we love him back with all of our heart, soul and strength!

Special Thanks

I want to extend a special thank you to Mandy Kelly, Rosilind Jukic, Bridget Childress and Misty Leask for your help with this journal. Your love, dedication and leadership to the Good Morning Girls ministry is such a blessing to all. Thank you for giving to the Lord.

~ Courtney

The Lord your God who goes before you

will Himself fight for you.

Deuteronomy 1:30

Reflection Question:

God blesses His people when they follow His commands. At times, we do our own thing and there are consequences for not being obedient.

How have you experienced this in your own life?

S—The S stands for *Scripture*

O—The O stands for *Observation*

A—The A stands for *Application*

K—The K stands for *Kneeling in Prayer*

For the Lord your God has blessed you in all the work of your hands. He knows your going through this great wilderness.

Deuteronomy 2:7

Reflection Question:

When God is on our side, there is no battle too big to fight.

Name a time when you faced a battle that God brought you through victoriously.

S—The S stands for *Scripture*

O—The O stands for *Observation*

A—The A stands for *Application*

K—The K stands for *Kneeling in Prayer*

You shall not fear them,

for it is the Lord your God

who fights for you.

Deuteronomy 3:22

Reflection Question:

Sometimes we give way to fear in the midst of life's battles. As a result, we miss out on seeing the work of God in our lives.

In what area of your life is God calling you to trust him more and not give in to your fears?

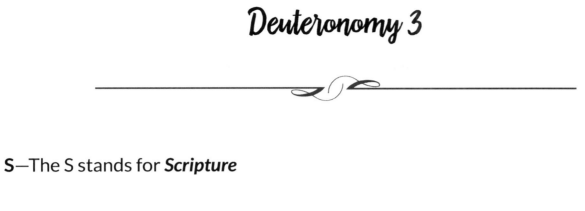

S—The S stands for *Scripture*

O—The O stands for *Observation*

A—The A stands for *Application*

K—The K stands for *Kneeling in Prayer*

For the Lord your God

is a consuming fire,

a jealous God.

Deuteronomy 4:24

Reflection Question:

God's mercy allows us to return to Him when we have walked away. He will never forsake us!

Name a time when you experienced God's mercy.

Deuteronomy 4

S—The S stands for *Scripture*

O—The O stands for *Observation*

A—The A stands for *Application*

K—The K stands for *Kneeling in Prayer*

You shall walk in all the ways

that the Lord your God has commanded you,

that it may go well with you,

and that you may live long in the land

that you shall possess.

Deuteronomy 5:33

Reflection Question:

God desires that we walk in all the ways that He commands, so that we may live well.

Which of the 10 commandments do you need to apply more in your life?

S—The S stands for *Scripture*

O—The O stands for *Observation*

A—The A stands for *Application*

K—The K stands for *Kneeling in Prayer*

You shall love the Lord your God

with all your heart

and with all your soul

and with all your might.

Deuteronomy 6:5

Reflection Question:

The greatest commandment is that we love God. When things are going well, it is easy to to lose our focus on Him and the blessings He gives.

What steps are you taking to ensure that God remains the focus of your life during the good and bad times?

Deuteronomy 6

S—The S stands for *Scripture*

O—The O stands for *Observation*

A—The A stands for *Application*

K—The K stands for *Kneeling in Prayer*

You shall not be in dread of them,

for the Lord your God is in your midst,

a great and awesome God.

Deuteronomy 7:21

Reflection Question:

Our God is mighty. We have no need to be afraid of those who stand against us.

How have you seen the mightiness of God at work in your life?

Deuteronomy 7

S—The S stands for *Scripture*

O—The O stands for *Observation*

A—The A stands for *Application*

K—The K stands for *Kneeling in Prayer*

Beware lest you say in your heart,

'My power and the might of my hand

have gotten me this wealth.'

You shall remember the Lord your God,

for it is he who gives you power to get wealth.

Deuteronomy 8:17,18

Reflection Question:

We must thank God for all that He does for us and not take credit for ourselves.

What do you need to thank God for doing in your life today?

Deuteronomy 8

S—The S stands for *Scripture*

O—The O stands for *Observation*

A—The A stands for *Application*

K—The K stands for *Kneeling in Prayer*

Know therefore today

that he who goes over before you

as a consuming fire

is the Lord your God.

Deuteronomy 9:3

Reflection Question:

Our sin should bring us to our knees before the Lord.

Take time to examine your heart and repent of any unconfessed sin in your life.

S—The S stands for *Scripture*

O—The O stands for *Observation*

A—The A stands for *Application*

K—The K stands for *Kneeling in Prayer*

What does the Lord your God require of you,

but to fear the Lord your God,

to walk in all his ways,

to love him, to serve the Lord your God

with all your heart and with all your soul.

Deuteronomy 10:12

Reflection Question:

God requires us to fear Him, walk in His ways, love Him and serve Him with all our hearts and souls.

In what ways are you living this out each day?

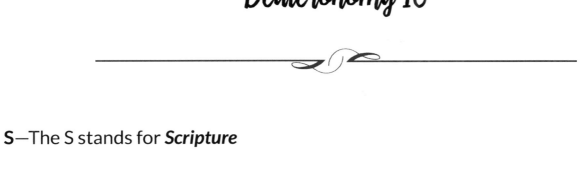

S—The S stands for *Scripture*

O—The O stands for *Observation*

A—The A stands for *Application*

K—The K stands for *Kneeling in Prayer*

Take care lest your heart be deceived,

and you turn aside and serve other gods

and worship them.

Deuteronomy 11:16

Reflection Question:

God warned the Israelites to pay attention, lest their hearts be deceived.

Have you been deceived in the past? How are you paying attention now, so that you will not be deceived?

S—The S stands for *Scripture*

O—The O stands for *Observation*

A—The A stands for *Application*

K—The K stands for *Kneeling in Prayer*

Everything that I command you,

you shall be careful to do.

You shall not add to it or take from it.

Deuteronomy 12:32

Reflection Question:

God's commandments must be followed, we cannot add to them nor take away from them.

How do you ensure that you're following God's commandments without adding or taking away from them?

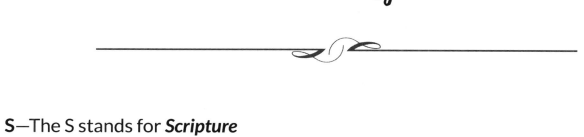

S—The S stands for *Scripture*

O—The O stands for *Observation*

A—The A stands for *Application*

K—The K stands for *Kneeling in Prayer*

You shall walk after the Lord your God
and fear him and keep his commandments
and obey his voice, and you shall serve him
and hold fast to him.

Deuteronomy 13:4

Reflection Question:

We must take care and compare all men's words to God's Word, in order to have the truth revealed.

Have you ever had a man's words not match up to God's Word? How did you handle that situation?

S—The S stands for *Scripture*

O—The O stands for *Observation*

A—The A stands for *Application*

K—The K stands for *Kneeling in Prayer*

You shall tithe
all the yield of your seed
that comes from the field year by year.

Deuteronomy 14:22

Reflection Question:

All that we have belongs to God.

How are you giving back to the Lord?

Deuteronomy 14

S—The S stands for *Scripture*

O—The O stands for *Observation*

A—The A stands for *Application*

K—The K stands for *Kneeling in Prayer*

You shall not harden your heart

or shut your hand

against your poor brother,

Deuteronomy 15:7

Reflection Question:

That which God blesses us with, we must not withhold from using to help those in need.

How can you reach out and bless someone in need today?

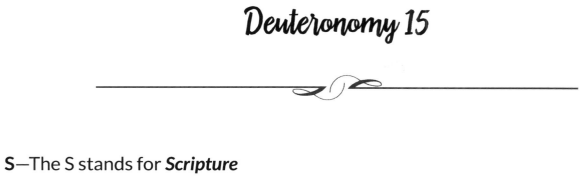

S—The S stands for *Scripture*

O—The O stands for *Observation*

A—The A stands for *Application*

K—The K stands for *Kneeling in Prayer*

Every man shall give as he is able,

according to the blessing

of the Lord your God

that he has given you.

Deuteronomy 16:17

Reflection Question:

Everything we have is a blessing from God. We need to have a willing heart to give back to Him.

How are you giving back to the Lord? How has this changed your life?

S—The S stands for *Scripture*

O—The O stands for *Observation*

A—The A stands for *Application*

K—The K stands for *Kneeling in Prayer*

He shall read in it all the days of his life,

that he may learn to fear the Lord his God

by keeping all the words of this law

and these statutes, and doing them.

Deuteronomy 17:19

Reflection Question:

We must read God's word daily so that we learn to fear the Lord and keep His ways.

How does having a daily Bible reading time, impact your life?

S—The S stands for *Scripture*

O—The O stands for *Observation*

A—The A stands for *Application*

K—The K stands for *Kneeling in Prayer*

You shall be blameless

before the Lord your God.

Deuteronomy 18:13

Reflection Question:

God's people were warned not to practice the customs of other nations. They were meant to be different.

How do you ensure that worldly influences don't influence your life?

S—The S stands for *Scripture*

O—The O stands for *Observation*

A—The A stands for *Application*

K—The K stands for *Kneeling in Prayer*

Purge the guilt

of innocent blood from Israel,

so that it may be well with you.

Deuteronomy 19:13

Reflection Question:

God provided refuge to those who had accidentally committed a sinful act.

How does this remind you of what He has done for you?

S—The S stands for *Scripture*

O—The O stands for *Observation*

A—The A stands for *Application*

K—The K stands for *Kneeling in Prayer*

Do not fear or panic

or be in dread of them,

for the Lord your God goes with you

to fight for you against your enemies,

to give you the victory.

Deuteronomy 20:3 & 4

Reflection Question:

God's people were reminded not to be afraid in times of battle because He was with them.

What battle have you faced and instantly you were scared until you remembered that God was with you?

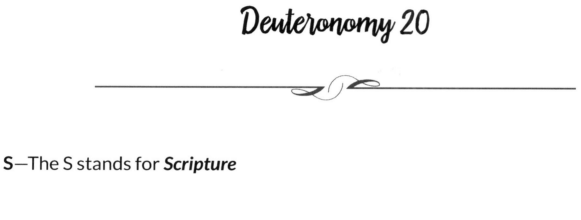

S—The S stands for *Scripture*

O—The O stands for *Observation*

A—The A stands for *Application*

K—The K stands for *Kneeling in Prayer*

Accept atonement, O Lord,

for your people Israel,

whom you have redeemed.

Deuteronomy 21:8

Reflection Question:

Provisions were made in the chance that guilty parties could not be found. This provision provided them with grace and redemption.

Name a problem in your life that you need to apply grace and mercy to.

Deuteronomy 21

S—The S stands for *Scripture*

O—The O stands for *Observation*

A—The A stands for *Application*

K—The K stands for *Kneeling in Prayer*

You shall purge the evil

from your midst.

Deuteronomy 22:21

Reflection Question:

Today we are reminded of the importance of remaining sexually pure both inside and outside of marriage.

In today's world, this can be a hard standard to live by. What are some ways that you have safeguarded yourself?

S—The S stands for *Scripture*

O—The O stands for *Observation*

A—The A stands for *Application*

K—The K stands for *Kneeling in Prayer*

If you make a vow

to the Lord your God,

you shall not delay fulfilling it,

for the Lord your God

will surely require it of you.

Deuteronomy 23:21

Reflection Question:

Vowing to God is very serious. Therefore, we need to be careful of the promises that we make to God.

Is there a vow that you have made to God that you are struggling to keep?

Deuteronomy 23

S—The S stands for *Scripture*

O—The O stands for *Observation*

A—The A stands for *Application*

K—The K stands for *Kneeling in Prayer*

You shall not oppress

a hired worker

who is poor and needy.

Deuteronomy 24:14

Reflection Question:

Providing for the less fortunate is commanded by God.

What are some ways you can help those around you?

S—The S stands for ***Scripture***

O—The O stands for ***Observation***

A—The A stands for ***Application***

K—The K stands for ***Kneeling in Prayer***

All who act dishonestly,

are an abomination

to the Lord your God.

Deuteronomy 25:16

Reflection Question:

In all our dealings, we must remain fair and honest. Otherwise, we are creating an act against God.

What are some ways that you can ensure that you are being fair, in all your dealings?

Deuteronomy 25

S—The S stands for *Scripture*

O—The O stands for *Observation*

A—The A stands for *Application*

K—The K stands for *Kneeling in Prayer*

You shall rejoice in all the good

that the Lord your God

has given to you and to your house.

Deuteronomy 26:11

Reflection Question:

We are to give to God and obey Him, with all our heart and soul.

What are some things or ways that you are tempted to hold back?

Deuteronomy 26

S—The S stands for *Scripture*

O—The O stands for *Observation*

A—The A stands for *Application*

K—The K stands for *Kneeling in Prayer*

You shall obey the voice
of the Lord your God,
keeping his commandments.

Deuteronomy 27:10

Reflection Question:

It is one thing to know God's commands; however, it's another thing to put them into action.

Do you sometimes struggle with this? What is it that causes you to stumble?

S—The S stands for *Scripture*

O—The O stands for *Observation*

A—The A stands for *Application*

K—The K stands for *Kneeling in Prayer*

All these blessings

shall come upon you

if you obey

the voice of the Lord your God.

Deuteronomy 28:2

Reflection Question:

God promised blessings to Israel for their obedience but curses for their disobedience.

Tell of a time when God blessed you for your obedience.

S—The S stands for *Scripture*

O—The O stands for *Observation*

A—The A stands for *Application*

K—The K stands for *Kneeling in Prayer*

The secret things belong to the LORD our God,

but the things that are revealed

belong to us and to our children forever,

that we may do all the words of this law.

Deuteronomy 29:29

Reflection Question:

God reveals through His Word, the things we need to know.

Name something God has recently revealed to you, through His Word.

Deuteronomy 29

S—The S stands for *Scripture*

O—The O stands for *Observation*

A—The A stands for *Application*

K—The K stands for *Kneeling in Prayer*

I have set before you life and death,

blessings and curses.

Therefore choose life,

that you and your offspring may live.

Deuteronomy 30:19

Reflection Question:

Today we are reminded that God wants and longs to bless his people because He loves us.

How does this simple truth make you feel? Have you shared your appreciation with God regarding all that He has blessed you with?

Deuteronomy 30

S—The S stands for *Scripture*

O—The O stands for *Observation*

A—The A stands for *Application*

K—The K stands for *Kneeling in Prayer*

Be strong and courageous.

Do not fear or be in dread of them,

for it is the Lord your God

who goes with you.

He will not leave you or forsake you.

Deuteronomy 31:6

Reflection Question:

Moses reminded the people that they have nothing to fear because God is with them and He will not leave them.

What is something that you need to lay at God's feet?

Deuteronomy 31

S—The S stands for *Scripture*

O—The O stands for *Observation*

A—The A stands for *Application*

K—The K stands for *Kneeling in Prayer*

He is the Rock, his work is perfect,

for all his ways are justice.

A God of faithfulness and without iniquity,

just and upright is he.

Deuteronomy 32:4

Reflection Question:

Moses encouraged the younger generation to ask the older generation about all God had brought them through.

Who can you share with, about all the things that God has brought you through?

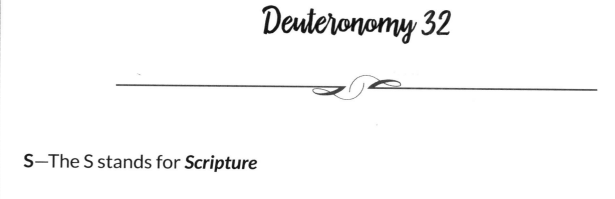

Deuteronomy 32

S—The S stands for *Scripture*

O—The O stands for *Observation*

A—The A stands for *Application*

K—The K stands for *Kneeling in Prayer*

The eternal God
is your dwelling place,
and underneath are His everlasting arms.

Deuteronomy 33:27

Reflection Question:

Moses left the people with encouraging words. God's people are blessed because they have God as their refuge.

How is God your refuge?

S—The S stands for *Scripture*

O—The O stands for *Observation*

A—The A stands for *Application*

K—The K stands for *Kneeling in Prayer*

There has not arisen a prophet since in Israel like Moses, whom the Lord knew face to face.

Deuteronomy 34:10

Reflection Question:

Moses died before they entered the Promise Land and yet he was at peace because he knew he had fulfilled his purpose.

What is God calling you to do? How are you fulfilling your purpose?

S—The S stands for *Scripture*

O—The O stands for *Observation*

A—The A stands for *Application*

K—The K stands for *Kneeling in Prayer*

Made in the USA
Lexington, KY
30 January 2017